new seasons®

New Seasons is a registered trademark of Publications International, Ltd.

Photography from: Jupiter Images and Shutterstock.com

Louis Weber, CEO
Publications International, Ltd.
8140 Lehigh Avenue
Morton Grove, IL 60053

**www.pilbooks.com**

Manufactured in Canada.

8  7  6  5  4  3  2  1

ISBN: 978-1-64030-712-4

# Mothers & Sons

Sometimes you need to run to mom.

Mom, when I look back at my life,
I can see how you were watching out
for me, even as you encouraged me to
tackle new challenges. Thank you.

You bring brightness to my life.

I saw how you took care of
our family, Mom, and I knew the
kind of person I wanted to be.

Moms help you find the keys to success.

It's my joy to see you fly.

Moms teach us how to dance.

Big brothers have big love.

Sometimes you need just to bundle up
and set off on an adventure.

You're my treasure.

I will always cheer you on.

Mommy, I brought you a present!

Shared laughter
brightens ordinary days.

Small happy moments
make treasured memories.

We may not have the same
taste in music, opinions, or ideas,
but I will always listen to what
you have to share.

A hug from Mom can't solve
every problem, but it can
make you feel better.

Mom, you showed me how to find balance in my life. Thanks.

Mom, what do you say we go
to the movies instead of school?

Mommy, I want what's in your bowl!

We make a pretty good team.

I love showing Grandpa and Grandma
how much you've grown!

Mom, thanks for teaching me
how to be a good friend.

Mom, I learned from you how
to care for Mother Earth.

Biggest supporter.
Finest audience.
Best Mom ever.

Before I decide to come
down...what's for dinner?

Someday you'll take the wheel,
but don't grow up too fast!

Mom, you're the best.

You don't think we look like pool sharks?
That's all part of our plan.

Wherever you go in life,
I'll always be wishing you
safe travel and smooth sailing.

You can handle this.
I have faith in you.

Looking back, I remember all
those times you held me up.
Thank you.

From you, Mom, I learned
when to color big and
bold outside the lines.

We first find safety, warmth, and love in a mother's arms.

Mom, you prepared me to
go out into the world
and take it by storm.

I don't know, Mom.
A hat *and* shoes *and* a smile
seem like a lot to ask.

You're getting bigger,
but you're still my little boy.

Sometimes we need to
share our awesomeness
with the world.

I love showing you the world.

I'll always remember your first steps.

No disguise can hide
how much I love you.

One of my joys is seeing the world anew through your eyes.

I wish for your happiness.

Mom, come on, the playground's this way.

It brought us joy when you came into our lives. It brings us joy that our family is growing again. We wish you joy through your life together.

Peekaboo! I love you!

Not bad, Mom. I'm still the master, though.

You're never too old
to listen to your mom.

You've got generations of love behind you.

Germs don't last.
The memories of Mom's TLC do.

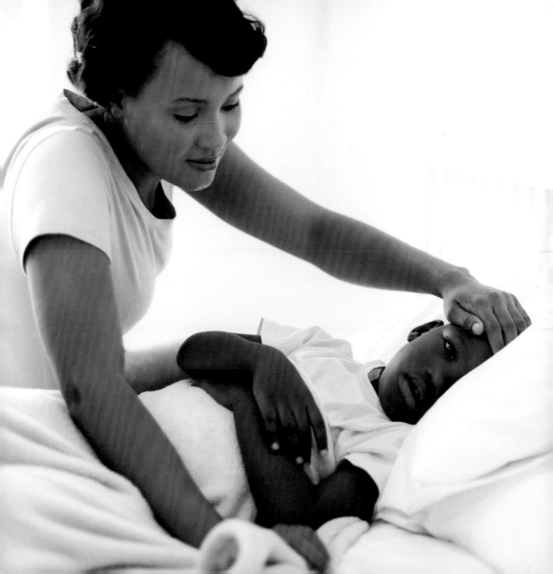

Mom, whenever I think
I know everything, I'm reminded of
how much you have to teach me.

I can always count on you to listen,
to understand, and to love.
Unconditionally.

When I need to hide out from
the world for a while, I go to Mom.